ESCAPE NORTH!
The Story of Harriet Tubman

SCHOLASTIC
ACTION™

Welcome to This Book

What would you do to be free? Would you risk your life? Would you risk your life to help others?

Harriet Tubman was born a slave. But one night she escaped. The trip was dangerous. But kind people helped her. They hid her from the slave catchers. They risked their lives, too. Once Harriet was free, she decided to go back. She wanted to help other people escape.

Why did she do this? Would Harriet get caught?

Target Words

These words will help you understand Harriet's story.

- **route:** a path from one place to another
  The Underground Railroad was a secret route for slaves from the South to escape to the North.

- **slavery:** keeping people as property
  Before the Civil War, slavery was legal in the South.

- **victory:** a win in a battle or contest
  Harriet Tubman helped win the victory over slavery.

Reader Tips

Here's how to get the most out of this book.

- **Illustrations** Look at the illustrations while you read. They'll help you understand the events in the story. Check out page 48 to see what Harriet Tubman really looked like.

- **Problem/Solution** Look for the main problem that Harriet has to face. Notice what she does to solve the problem. Knowing how Harriet solves her problem will help you better understand the story of her life.

For my mother
—M.K.

To Paige Gillies
—T.F.

With special thanks to Alice Adamczyk, of the Schomburg Center for Research in Black Culture, for her time and expertise in reviewing this book.

Text copyright © 2000 by Monica Kulling.
Illustrations copyright © 2000 by Teresa Flavin.
All rights reserved. Published by Scholastic Inc., 557 Broadway, New York, NY 10012, by arrangement with Random House Children's Books, a division of Random House, Inc.
Printed in the U.S.A.

ISBN 0-439-58896-0

5 6 7 8 9 10   23   12 11 10 09 08 07

ESCAPE NORTH!
The Story of Harriet Tubman

Wilmington
Shoe shop

NEW JERSEY

Brodas
Plantation

born 1820

MARYLAND

Safe houses
Camden

DELAWARE

by Monica Kulling
illustrated by Teresa Flavin

SCHOLASTIC INC.
New York Toronto London Auckland Sydney
Mexico City New Delhi Hong Kong Buenos Aires

Contents

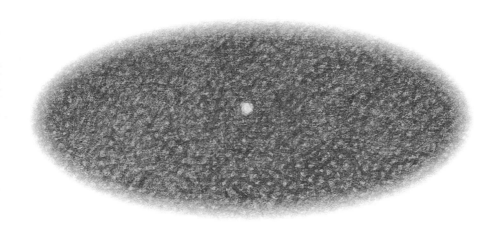

1
Escape North!

The night was dark. Cricket song filled the air. A woman hid outside a cabin. She whistled a song called "Go Down, Moses." A line in the song said: "Let my people go."

Inside the cabin, the slaves knew that Harriet Tubman had come to lead her people out of slavery.

It was 1851. Harriet Tubman was a conductor on the Underground Railroad. The Underground Railroad wasn't a *real* railroad. It was the name people gave the route taking slaves north to freedom.

Years before, a slave had run off. He had seemed to disappear right in front of his owner's eyes.

"He must have gone on an underground railroad," said the owner.

The story spread. There was a way
north to the free states! There were people
who would help. They would hide you in
their homes. These safe houses were
stations on the Underground Railroad.
Runaways ran from station to station until
they reached a state where slavery was
against the law.

That Saturday night, ten slaves answered Harriet's call to freedom. Field slaves had Sundays off, so the bossman wouldn't know they were gone until Monday. Then he and his dogs would come after them. If they were caught, they would be beaten…maybe to death.

Harriet was there to make sure that didn't happen. She kept her eyes on one star in the sky—the North Star. She moved quickly, and the runaways followed.

Suddenly, clouds covered the star. Harriet had to make sure she was heading in the right direction. If she didn't, they could end up back at the plantation!

Harriet ran her fingers over the bark of the tree nearest her. Daddy Ben had taught her that moss grew on the north side of trees.

I'll have to find north the way my daddy taught me, she thought.

Harriet closed her eyes and thought back to the lessons of long ago. She thought back to when she was a girl.

2
Born a Slave

Harriet Tubman was born Araminta Ross in about 1820. As a child, she was called Minty. Later, she took the name Harriet, after her mother, who was called Old Rit.

Harriet was born a slave on a tobacco plantation in Maryland. She and her family were the property of a man named Edward Brodas. That meant they had little say over their own lives. They could even be sold and separated from each other.

Harriet's family lived in a small cabin near the master's house. It had no windows and only a bare earth floor. The family slept on beds made of straw. They used rags for blankets. They didn't have much to eat.

Harriet didn't go to school. Slaves weren't allowed to learn to read or write.

Instead, she helped her mother cook.

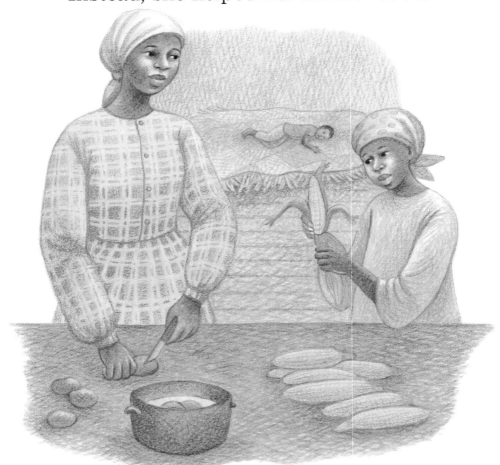

She carried buckets of water to the slaves working in the fields.

She picked insects off tobacco plants.

When Harriet was seven, she was sent to work for a neighbor, Mrs. Cook. Mrs. Cook made Harriet wind yarn all day. Sometimes the yarn broke. Then Mrs. Cook got out the whip.

"You stupid girl," she yelled. "I'll show you what real work is."

Mrs. Cook sent Harriet to work for Mr. Cook. Day after day, Harriet stood in the swamp, checking muskrat traps. Finally, she got sick, and Mr. Cook took her home.

When she was well, Mr. Brodas sent
her into the tobacco fields.

In the fields, slaves worked long hours
in the hot sun. If they didn't work fast
enough, they were beaten. It didn't seem

fair to Harriet. Sometimes, she looked up at
the sky and watched the birds flying
north. She promised herself that one day
she too would fly north to freedom.

3
The Accident

When Harriet was a teenager, a slave
working in the fields ran off. The bossman
threw a weight at him to stop him. But it
hit Harriet instead.

Harriet wasn't the same after that. She
fell asleep without warning. Sometimes her
head would drop in the middle of a sentence
and she would be asleep.

These sleeping spells made escape even
more dangerous. But Harriet's mind was
made up.

Daddy Ben, her father, knew Harriet would run. He wanted her to make it when she did. He showed Harriet where to hide in the woods. He showed her which plants and berries were safe to eat. He taught her how to run quickly and silently through the forest.

Most important, he taught Harriet how to find north.

"See that Big Dipper in the sky," said Daddy Ben one evening.

Harriet picked out the stars that formed a dipping ladle.

"See that bright star above the bowl?" asked Daddy Ben. "That's the North Star. Follow it and you'll be heading toward freedom."

4
Harriet Escapes

Years went by. Whenever Harriet lost heart, she looked up at the North Star.

When she was twenty-eight, Harriet fell in love with John Tubman. Slaves weren't allowed to marry. So they "jumped the broom" instead. A broom was laid on the floor. The couple jumped over it. When they landed, they were husband and wife.

Harriet told John her plan to escape. "I have a right to freedom or death," she said. "I will have one or the other, since no one is going to bring me back alive."

John didn't want trouble. He said he would tell Mr. Brodas if Harriet kept talking about running away.

Harriet stopped talking about it, but she didn't stop thinking about it.

One day, Harriet found out that she had
been sold. It was time to act!

Weeks before, a Quaker woman had
offered to help. Quakers were religious
people who believed that owning another
human being was wrong. The woman gave
Harriet directions to a safe house in
Delaware, the next state over.

The next Saturday, Harriet waited until John was asleep. She wrapped cornbread and salt herring in a handkerchief. She silently opened the cabin door.

Outside, the North Star pointed the way. Harriet didn't look back. She took off into the woods, running fast!

5
Free at Last!

Harriet ran for hours. Sharp pains stabbed her sides. But she didn't stop.

She followed the Choptank River to the Maryland border. As she ran, Harriet remembered Daddy Ben's words:

"Walk through water when you can. The dogs will lose your scent."

Harriet took off her shoes and stepped into the icy river. When the sun rose, she

heard the baying of hounds. The bossman
was on her trail!

Harriet found a small island in a
swamp. She hid in a hollow log. She was
so tired, she fell asleep. She didn't hear the
slave catchers galloping past.

In Camden, Delaware, Harriet found
the safe house the Quaker woman had told
her about. A brightly colored quilt hung on
the clothesline. That meant it was safe for
Harriet to knock.

The owners welcomed Harriet into their home. They fed her. They hid her in the attic, where she slept all day. When night came, Harriet thanked them and ran for the next safe house.

Once, Harriet fell asleep on the road.
She woke up just as a group of slave
hunters were approaching. Harriet
scrambled into a ditch and covered herself
with mud. She prayed the hunters wouldn't
see her. Somehow, they never did.

After days of running, Harriet crossed into the free state of Pennsylvania. She looked at her hands. She was the same person. But something about her had changed. Her hands belonged to *her* now, not to anyone else. Harriet Tubman was free!

In Philadelphia, Harriet found a room
to rent. She found work as a cook in a
hotel. One day she met a man named
William Still. He was the secretary of the
American Anti-Slavery Society. Harriet
went to the society's secret meetings.

One night at a meeting, Harriet found out that her sister's family had escaped. They were hiding in Baltimore. They needed someone to lead them to safety.

"I will lead them," said Harriet.

The men at the meeting were shocked. There were no women conductors on the Underground Railroad.

It was too dangerous.

But Harriet would not be swayed. She was going to free her people, just like Moses in the Bible.

6
No Turning Back

That first trip had been long ago. Harriet
remembered it now as she felt the moss on
the tree. She had made it then, and she
would make it again. "This way!" she told
the runaways.

Finally, the group reached a safe house. But the stationmaster wouldn't let them in. He was afraid of the Fugitive Slave Act. The new law said that anyone helping runaways could be severely punished.

Harriet led the group back into the woods. Everyone was tired and hungry. One woman was so weak that Harriet had to carry her.

Suddenly, one of the men stopped. "I'm going back," he said. "It's better to be a slave than suffer like this."

Harriet stood in his way. If the slave catchers caught him, they would beat the secrets of the Underground Railroad out of him. Harriet couldn't let that happen.

She pointed her gun at the man.

"You run back and you'll never run again," she said. "Come with me now or die."

The group trudged on.

Finally, they found a safe house in
Wilmington, Delaware. A Quaker named
Thomas Garrett owned a shoe store. He

had a secret room for runaways to hide in
behind a wall of shoe boxes. When the
runaways were ready to leave, he gave
them each a pair of shoes.

When they reached Philadelphia, William Still gave Harriet money to take the group on to Canada.

He wrote in his journal:

"Harriet Tubman is not afraid. The idea that she could be caught at any time doesn't seem to enter her mind."

7
Saving Daddy Ben and Old Rit

Daddy Ben and Old Rit were now in their seventies. Running would be hard for them. But Harriet wanted her parents to know freedom.

In 1857, she went back to Maryland dressed as an old woman. Daddy Ben and Old Rit were overjoyed to see her.

Harriet took an old horse and wagon
from a nearby plantation. That night,
Daddy Ben and Old Rit climbed into the
back of the wagon. Harriet covered them
with blankets.

She drove the horse as fast as she could. She wanted to be out of Maryland by daybreak.

In Delaware, a Quaker railroad agent sold them train tickets.

Daddy Ben and Old Rit could hardly believe it. They had been slaves all their lives. Now Harriet was using Daddy Ben's lessons to bring them to freedom.

8
Harriet's Last Years

In 1861, the Civil War broke out. President Abraham Lincoln wanted to free the slaves. But the Southern states were against this. One by one, they left the Union. They formed a union of their own, called the Confederacy.

The war tore the country apart.

As always, Harriet was quick to join the fight. She worked as a spy and a scout for the North. She also worked as a nurse.

In 1865, the North won the Civil War. The Underground Railroad stopped running. The fight to free the slaves was over.

Harriet spent her later years in Auburn, New York, taking care of her parents. After many years, the government decided to give her a reward for her work. She used the money to build a home for elderly blacks who had no place to live.

In 1913, Harriet became too sick to get out of bed. Visitors read the newspaper to her. She followed the news of women fighting for the right to vote. She sent them a message: "Stand together."

It was a message that had helped her people win the victory over slavery. One day, it would help women win the vote.

Harriet died at the age of ninety-three. She had made at least nineteen trips south and brought more than three hundred people out of slavery. "I've never run a train off the track, and I've never lost a passenger," she liked to say. Today, Harriet Tubman is remembered as the "Moses of Her People" and one of the bravest soldiers in the fight against slavery.

Glossary

approach *(verb)* to move near (p. 30)

attic *(noun)* a space in a building that is just below the roof (p. 29)

cabin *(noun)* a small, simple wooden house (p. 5)

conductor *(noun)* someone who directs a train; in the Underground Railroad, a conductor guided the slaves to safety (p. 6)

journal *(noun)* a diary in which you write thoughts and experiences (p. 40)

muskrat *(noun)* a small rodent with webbed feet that lives in and around water (p. 15)

plantation *(noun)* a large farm where crops are grown; before the Civil War, Southern plantations were often worked by slaves (p. 9)

route *(noun)* a path from one place to another (p. 6)

safe house *(noun)* a safe place for slaves traveling on the Underground Railroad (p. 7)

scramble *(verb)* to move quickly (p. 30)

severely *(adverb)* harshly (p. 35)

slavery *(noun)* keeping people as property (p. 5)

station *(noun)* a place where passengers get on or off a train; slaves hid in stations, or people's homes, as they escaped north (p. 7)

trudge *(verb)* to walk with great effort (p. 36)

Underground Railroad *(noun)* a chain of people who secretly helped slaves from the South escape to the free North or Canada before the Civil War (p. 6)

victory *(noun)* a win in a battle or contest (p. 47)

Index

A

American Anti-Slavery
  Society 32, 33

B

bossman 8, 18, 27
Brodas, Edward 11, 16, 23

C

Canada 40
Civil War 44
conductor(s) 6, 33
Confederacy 44

D

Daddy Ben 10, 21, 26, 41–43
Delaware 24, 28, 38, 43

F

free state(s) 7, 31
freedom 6, 17, 21, 23, 41, 43
Fugitive Slave Act 35

G

Garrett, Thomas 38

L

Lincoln, Abraham 44

M

Maryland 11, 26, 41, 43
Moses 33, 48

N

North Star 9, 21–22, 25

O

Old Rit 11, 41–43

P

Pennsylvania 31
Philadelphia 32, 40
plantation 9, 11, 42

Q

Quaker 24, 28, 38, 43

R

Ross, Araminta 11
route 6
runaways 9, 34–35, 39